EARTH MOVERS™

Bulldozers

Joanne Randolph

The Rosen Publishing Group's
PowerKids Press™
New York

For Ryan, with love

Published in 2002 by The Rosen Publishing Group, Inc.
29 East 21st Street, New York, NY 10010

First Edition

Book Design: Michael Donnellan

Photo Credits: p. 5 © CORBIS; p. 7 © CORBIS/Roger Ressmeyer; pp. 9, 11, 15, 15, and 19 © CORBIS/Raymond Gehman; p. 13 © Highway Images/ Bette S. Garber; p. 17 © Highway Images/Genat; p. 21 © Index Stock.

Randolph, Joanne.
Bulldozers / Joanne Randolph.— 1st ed.
     p. cm. — (Earth movers)
Includes bibliographical references and index.
ISBN 0-8239-6025-0
1. Bulldozers—Juvenile literature. [1. Bulldozers.] I. Title.
TA735 .R36 2002
629.225—dc21
                                            00-013013

Manufactured in the United States of America

Contents

This is a bulldozer.

Bulldozers are big.

Bulldozers clear land.
Bulldozers push rocks,
dirt, and trees out
of the way.

9

A bulldozer has a big metal blade on the front. The blade pushes the rocks, dirt, and trees.

Some bulldozers have
a ripper on the back.
The ripper tears up the
ground with its teeth.

13

A bulldozer does
not have tires.
It has crawler tracks.
Crawler tracks help the
bulldozer drive over
bumpy ground.

A person drives the bulldozer. The driver moves the ripper and blade up and down.

17

Bulldozers are very important machines. They help build roads and houses.

A bulldozer might have helped to build the roads you use every day.

21

Words to Know

blade

bulldozer

crawler tracks

ripper

Here are more books to read about bulldozers:

Mighty Machines: Truck
By Claire Llewellyn
Dorling Kindersley Publishing

Diggers and Dump Trucks
(Eye Openers)
By Angela Royston
Little Simon

To learn more about bulldozers, check out this Web site:
www.komatsu.co.jp/kikki/zukan/e_index.htm

Index

Word Count: 113
Note to Librarians, Teachers, and Parents

PowerKids Readers are specially designed to help emergent and beginning readers build their skills in reading for information. Simple vocabulary and concepts are paired with photographs of real kids in real-life situations or stunning, detailed images from the natural world around them. Readers will respond to written language by linking meaning with their own everyday experiences and observations. Sentences are short and simple, employing a basic vocabulary of sight words, as well as new words that describe objects or processes that take place in the natural world. Large type, clean design, and photographs corresponding directly to the text all help children to decipher meaning. Features such as a contents page, picture glossary, and index help children get the most out of PowerKids Readers. They also introduce children to the basic elements of a book, which they will encounter in their future reading experiences. Lists of related books and Web sites encourage kids to explore other sources and to continue the process of learning.